Julia Gonzaga

by Simonetta Carr

with Illustrations by Matt Abraxas

REFORMATION HERITAGE BOOKS

Grand Rapids, Michigan

Julia Gonzaga
© 2019 by Simonetta Carr
Cover artwork by Matt Abraxas
For additional artwork by Matt, see pages 7, 11, 15, 19, 23, 29, 31, 37, 41, 43, 51, 53.

Reformation Heritage Books
2965 Leonard St. NE
Grand Rapids, MI 49525
616-977-0889
e-mail: orders@heritagebooks.org
website: www.heritagebooks.org

Printed in the United States of America
19 20 21 22 23 24/10 9 8 7 6 5 4 3 2 1

Library of Congress Cataloging-in-Publication Data

Names: Carr, Simonetta, author. | Abraxas, Matt, illustrator.
Title: Julia Gonzaga / by Simonetta Carr ; with illustrations by Matt Abraxas.
Description: Grand Rapids, Michigan : Reformation Heritage Books, [2019] | Series: Christian biographies for young readers | Audience: Ages 7-12.
Identifiers: LCCN 2018054875 | ISBN 9781601786784 (hardcover : alk. paper)
Subjects: LCSH: Gonzaga-Colonna, Giulia di, duchessa di Traetto, 1513?-1566 —Juvenile literature. | Nobility—Italy—Biography—Juvenile literature. | Reformation—Italy—Juvenile literature. | Inquisition—Italy—Juvenile literature. | Italy—Church history—16th century—Juvenile literature. | Italy—History—16th century—Juvenile literature.
Classification: LCC DG540.8.G6 C37 2019 | DDC 282.092 [B] —dc23 LC record available at https://lccn.loc.gov/2018054875

For additional Reformed literature, request a free book list from Reformation Heritage Books at the above address.

CHRISTIAN BIOGRAPHIES FOR YOUNG READERS

This series introduces children to important people in the Christian tradition. Parents and schoolteachers alike will welcome the excellent educational value it provides for students, while the quality of the publication and the artwork make each volume a keepsake for generations to come. Furthermore, the books in the series go beyond the simple story of someone's life by teaching young readers the historical and theological relevance of each character.

AVAILABLE VOLUMES OF THE SERIES
John Calvin
Augustine of Hippo
John Owen
Athanasius
Lady Jane Grey
Anselm of Canterbury
John Knox
Jonathan Edwards
Marie Durand
Martin Luther
Peter Martyr Vermigli
Irenaeus of Lyon
John Newton
Julia Gonzaga

Table of Contents

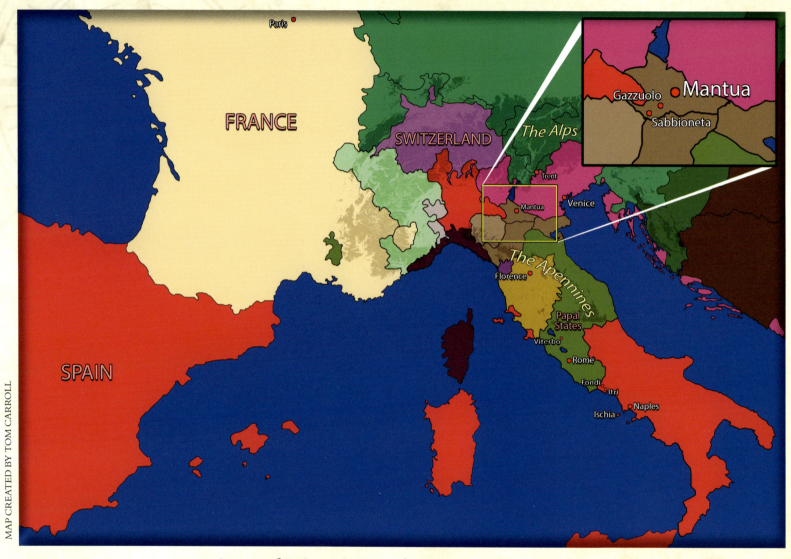

FRANCE

SWITZERLAND

The Alps

Trent

Venice

Mantua

Gazzuolo

Sabbioneta

Mantua

SPAIN

The Apennines

Florence

Papal
States

Viterbo

Rome

Fondi
Itri

Ischia

Naples

Paris

A map of Italy and parts of Europe during Julia's life

Introduction

At age twenty, Julia Gonzaga was already one of the most envied women in Italy. She owned large properties, and her castle was a favorite meeting place for artists, poets, and musicians. She was considered the prettiest woman in the country. Yet she was anxious and confused.

She knew that God hates and punishes sin, but she usually ended up disobeying Him anyway, she said, because she cared too much about the opinions of others. Sometimes she would go against her conscience in order to please others and avoid offending them. No matter how much she tried, sooner or later she would put these fears and desires before obeying God.

She finally found peace a few years later when someone helped her understand how the gospel could both bring forgiveness and give her the power to obey. After that, she devoted her life to spreading the same good news to others.

Julia Gonzaga
SCALA/ART RESOURCE

CHAPTER ONE
A Young Girl and Young Bride

Julia was born in 1513 in the small town of Gazzuolo (gah-TSWOH-loh), in northern Italy, to Count Ludovico (loo-doh-VEE-koh) and his wife, Francesca (frahn-CHEHS-kah). Like most Italian noblemen of his time, Count Ludovico was an army captain who offered his services where they were needed and trained most of his sons to follow in his footsteps. The Gonzaga (gond-ZAH-gah) family was well known and respected—an offshoot of a larger family who ruled Mantua. Over the years they had kept a lively court composed of about one hundred people—secretaries, administrators, cooks, guards, tutors, and servants—and attended by artists, writers, and musicians.

Julia was the youngest of eleven children. Her favorite brother was the oldest—Luigi (loo-EE-jee), nicknamed "Rodomonte" after a powerful hero of an Italian epic poem. Luigi was thirteen years older than Julia. Once, during one of their frequent visits to the rich court of their relatives in Mantua, seven-year-old Julia was nominated to be queen of a tournament (a competition of knights) and had the honor of crowning Luigi as the winner.

Seven-year-old Julia was nominated to be queen of a tournament and had the honor of crowning her brother Luigi as the winner.

Most of the time, however, she stayed home with her mother, grandmother, and five sisters. As was typical of girls in noble families, she learned to read, write, sing, dance, and embroider. One of the family tutors thought she was the most talented and studious of the Gonzaga girls.

In those days, especially in influential families, parents and relatives arranged their children's marriages, and Julia knew that this was what the future held for her. Normally the choice was based on what was best for the family. Julia's parents looked for a man in the Colonna (koh-LON-nah) family, which was both powerful and influential. They chose a man in his forties named Vespasiano (ves-pah-ZEEAH-noh), whose wife had recently died, leaving him with a daughter, Isabella. Julia and Isabella were about the same age. It must have been strange for thirteen-year-old Julia to become the stepmother of another teenage girl.

Coat of arms of the Gonzaga family

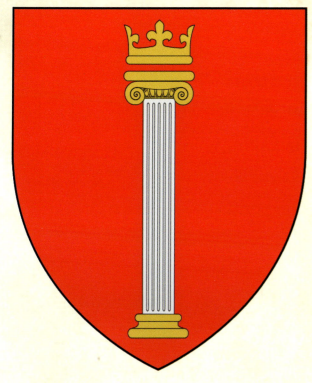

Coat of arms of the Colonna family

WIKIMEDIA COMMONS

Vespasiano and Julia's wedding was celebrated in July 1526. We don't know how Julia felt about it, but she didn't have a choice. In any case, Vespasiano was a military captain and was gone to battle most of the time, leaving Julia and Isabella in one of his castles.

As he was in poor health, Vespasiano died on March 13, 1528, less than two years after his wedding. Before dying, he wrote his last will. All his property was to go to Julia, as long as she remained unmarried. If she ever married again, everything would go to Isabella. This decision shocked many people. Normally all properties were left to the men in the family.

CHAPTER TWO

A Teenage Ruler

Julia, then fifteen, was left to rule alone over her husband's territories. Knowing that someone could take advantage of the situation, she asked her brothers for help. Luigi, who had become influential during the recent wars, was especially helpful, persuading neighboring noblemen to protect her lands.

Julia and Isabella moved to Vespasiano's castle in Fondi, a small city in a fertile, hilly area. The castle, surrounded by a large orange grove, was in a convenient position between the cities of Naples and Rome and attracted many visitors. Some were men and women of the nobility looking for a place to stop along the way, but many came just to see Julia, who had gained a reputation for being a supporter of the arts, surrounding herself with painters, writers, and musicians. Given her beauty, many men dreamed of marrying her, but she was not interested in marriage.

SABIEN MOUS, FLICKR

Castle of Fondi

Julia surrounded herself with painters, writers, and musicians.

According to Vespasiano's will, Julia had the duty of organizing Isabella's wedding. Vespasiano had already chosen a husband for Isabella: a young nobleman named Ippolito de' Medici (ip-POHL-ee-toh DEH MEY-dee-chee). Vespasiano had given Julia permission to arrange a marriage with one of her brothers if for some reason a marriage with Ippolito couldn't work out.

As it turns out, the marriage didn't work out because Ippolito's uncle, Pope Clement VIII, appointed him as cardinal, a position that was only one step lower than the pope. In those days, it was rare for young people to go against their family's wishes. In Ippolito's case, the order had even greater authority because it was given by the pope, head of the Roman Catholic Church—the only type of church in Italy—and ruler over much of the country.

Ippolito de' Medici

SCALA/MINISTERO PER I BENI E LE ATTIVITÀ CULTURALI /ART RESOURCE

Luigi "Rodomonte" Gonzaga

In the Roman Catholic Church, cardinals—like priests, bishops, and monks—could not get married, so Julia and her family agreed that Isabella should marry Luigi. Isabella must have been happy because Luigi was handsome, generous, intelligent, and brave. The couple loved each other very much. They got married in 1531 in Rome.

Julia asked the newlyweds to live in her castle, where Luigi could defend the property and help her rule. The following year, when the couple had a child, she enjoyed being an aunt. "God graced us with a son," she wrote. The boy was named Vespasiano, after his grandfather. But Julia's joy didn't last long because the following year Luigi was shot to death while protecting her lands from an enemy attack. Both Julia and Isabella were heartbroken.

CHAPTER THREE
Danger and Sorrow

Following Luigi's wishes, Isabella and Vespasiano went to live with Luigi's father, while Julia continued to oversee her large properties alone, traveling with her guards even to dangerous areas along the Apennine Mountains. She was a good administrator and was able to enjoy a few years of peace—until the summer of 1534, when a band of pirates raided the Italian coast, moving from Sicily up toward Rome. Their leader was Khayr Al-Din (KAIR al-DEEN), known to Italians as Barbarossa (Red Beard). These pirates were fierce. Wherever they went, they spoiled cities, burned buildings, killed people, and took slaves.

During the night of August 8, 1534, they arrived in Fondi and entered Julia's castle, capturing all its goods, including valuables the townspeople had hidden there for safety. Having heard about Julia's beauty, Khayr Al-Din decided to kidnap her as a present to Grand Sultan Suleiman (SOO-lay-mon) I, ruler of the large Turkish Empire. Julia managed to escape from a window, still barefoot and in her nightgown, and rode her horse to safety while her castle's main tower burned in the distance.

Pirate Khayr Al-Din, "Barbarossa," as portrayed by a contemporary artist

Julia managed to escape the pirates' attack by jumping barefoot out of a window and riding her horse to safety.

In the meantime, the news of the pirates' raids had reached the pope, who, as ruler of a large region just above Fondi, asked Ippolito to lead an army against them. Ippolito must have been glad to help Julia because he had always loved her. In the end, Khayr Al-Din and his men moved to Tunisia, in North Africa, where they were defeated by Charles V, emperor of the Germanic states.

Julia returned to Fondi to find dreadful destruction. Besides the huge loss of valuables, over one thousand houses had been damaged, churches had been robbed, 73 people (including children) had been killed, and 150 had been taken as slaves. The surrounding area had suffered similar losses. She must have been shaken and uncertain about her ability

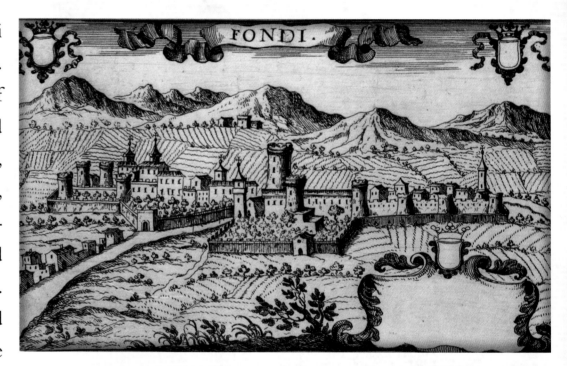

Fondi in a seventeenth-century print
FONDO ANTIGUO DE LA BIBLIOTECA DE LA UNIVERSIDAD DE SEVILLA

to protect her lands. At the same time, she had to deal with demands by Isabella, who had returned to her own family and hired lawyers to take her father's properties from Julia. In fact, there were rumors that Isabella's family had made an agreement with the pirates to kidnap Julia.

The following year, Ippolito traveled to Naples to meet Emperor Charles V, who was going to stop in that city as he returned from Tunisia. As the most powerful ruler in Europe, Charles had a strong influence on small Italian states. Ippolito and many others in Florence hoped that Charles, who had placed the Medici family back in power five years earlier, could depose their tyrannical Medici ruler, Alessandro.

On his way south, Ippolito stopped at Julia's castle of Itri, where he visited with her. His stay was not pleasant because he fell suddenly and violently ill.

The castle at Itri

MM, WIKIMEDIA COMMONA

**Bronze coin portraying
Alessandro de' Medici**

NATIONAL GALLERY OF ART,
SAMUEL H. KRESS COLLECTION

The illness might have been malaria, a disease carried by mosquitoes especially in swampy areas like the countryside south of Rome. Some people thought Ippolito was poisoned by men hired by Alessandro de' Medici. In fact, Ippolito remembered that his soup had a strange taste. In any case, he died after a few days of terrible suffering. Julia comforted him as much as she could. He was only twenty-four, and Julia twenty-two.

Ippolito's death was a traumatic experience for Julia. Since her husband's death, she had lost two other men who had been her most capable defenders: Luigi and Ippolito. This might be why she decided to move to Naples, Italy, leaving her properties in the hands of her administrators.

Julia was able to comfort Ippolito as he died.

CHAPTER FOUR
A Change of Heart

Initially, Julia's trip to Naples was meant to be short-term. She was just supposed to represent her family in discussing some urgent matters with Charles V. While doing so, she stayed in a small area inside a convent of nuns. After a while, she found the accommodation so pleasant that she decided to live there for good.

Staying with nuns was a common choice for widows like Julia because convents offered protection and support. Her lodging was much smaller than any of her castles, but it was still large enough to house a few servants and receive friends. She also kept another house in Naples where she could host visitors for longer periods of time.

NATIONAL GALLERY OF ART, ROSENWALD COLLECTION

Emperor Charles V, as portrayed by a contemporary artist

At that time, Naples was a prosperous city and a center of literature and art. There, Julia had several friends. One of them was Juan de Valdés (hwahn deh val-DEHZ), a Spanish nobleman who had been helping her resolve her legal disagreement with Isabella. Valdés had been forced to leave Spain because of his religious beliefs. Like many other people at that time, he wanted to see the church come closer to biblical teachings and abandon some traditions that were not in the Bible. Most church authorities, however, were not ready to change and did everything in their power to stop people like Valdés. Valdés found some protection in Italy, where his brother, who worked for the emperor, found him a respected position.

In spite of his training in law, Valdés couldn't help Julia because the emperor became involved, awarding Vespasiano's properties to Isabella and allowing Julia to keep only a yearly salary. It was not a fair sentence because Vespasiano had left everything to Julia, but she could not prove it because his will had been destroyed during the pirates' attack.

Map of sixteenth-century Naples

Isabella was not completely happy either, because the emperor had ordered her to remarry. According to the laws of that time, a widow who remarried had to leave her children with the family of their father—in this case, Isabella had to leave little Vespasiano with Julia's father. This made her resent Julia even more, and she often tried to avoid sending Julia the salary she owed her.

On most Sundays, Julia attended the small church next to the convent. The week before Easter, instead, she decided to listen to a famous preacher, Bernardino Ochino (oh-KEY-noh), who had just arrived in town. Ochino was a small, thin man who spoke in a soft voice. His words, however, were so powerful that the emperor thought they could draw tears from statues of stone.

It was not the first time that Julia heard Ochino preach. Initially, his sermons had given her peace, but eventually they started to have the opposite effect, causing all kinds of questions and fears. After church, she decided to share her uncertainties with Valdés.

After church, Julia shared her uncertainties with her friend Juan de Valdés.

The two talked for a while in front of the church, then continued their discussion at her residence. Her problem, she said, is that preachers encouraged listeners to examine their hearts, but hers was full of disobedience to God. "Normally, I feel so dissatisfied about myself and everything in this world," she told Valdés, "and so sluggish that if you could see my heart I am sure you would be moved with compassion, filled as it is with confusion, puzzlement, and unrest."

Many people felt the weight of their sins, and the Roman Catholic Church encouraged them to find remedy by confessing to a priest, saying long prayers, performing good works, and doing some sort of self-punishment like fasting. These measures made some people feel better but gave no relief to Julia. She knew they couldn't possibly be enough to remedy her offenses against God. But then, what was? How could she ever stop sinning and find favor with a God who says, "Be perfect" (Matthew 5:48)?

Valdés explained the problem. Since Adam and Eve first sinned, no human being has been able to obey completely because all human nature is now stained by sin. What's more, God, being both holy and just, can't ignore sin but has to punish it.

This would be terrible news, but God has provided a solution. He sent His Son as true man and true God to live a perfect life in sinners' place and take the punishment they deserve. The story of this plan of salvation is called the gospel.

It was important for Julia to see the difference between law and gospel. When the Bible tells us to do something, that is a law. When it tells us what Christ has done for us, that is the gospel. The law cannot save. It shows us what God requires and how far we have strayed. If we look at the law, we can become discouraged and scared, unless we immediately look at the gospel—the good news that Christ has perfectly obeyed that law for us and has freed us from the power of sin.

The discussion continued for hours, with many questions and answers. In the end, Julia understood God's promises of salvation better than ever before. She also understood that faith—a gift of God that can never be earned—takes God at His word. If Christ says that whoever believes in Him will be saved, faith trusts in that promise. That certainty gave Julia great peace.

After that day, she continued to talk with Valdés and with a group of his friends who met together to study the Bible—often in gardens or by the ocean. She also began sharing the gospel with the nuns at the convent where she was staying, and many of them believed.

Today's view of the ocean by the neighborhood of Chiaia (KYAH-yah), Naples, where Juan de Valdés lived and met his friends

FRANCO TIMPANARO, FLICKR

From time to time, Julia still visited the important families of Naples, where poets, artists, and musicians gathered, and joined them in their parties. She was particularly close to her Uncle Ferrante (fair-RAHN-tay) and his family and loved his children as her own. Most of the time, however, she stayed in the tranquility of the convent.

The nuns kept a garden and made delicious treats, as well as natural remedies, that Julia liked to send to her friends everywhere: sweets made with rose petals or almonds, marmalade made with citrons, a mixture of sugar and rose extract to fight mucous and promote sleep, and many more. She also exchanged recipes with her female friends.

Among other treats, Julia shared with her friends some typical Italian cookies known as mustaccioli (moos-tatch-CHOH-lee). They come in many variations.

In the meantime, Valdés kept teaching and writing. One of his first works was a written copy in Spanish of the long conversation he had shared with Julia. He called it *Christian Alphabet* because it included a basic knowledge of what the Bible teaches. He also translated the book of Psalms into Castilian (a version of Spanish) and wrote commentaries on the Psalms and most of the New Testament.

He also wrote a small book of religious instruction, called a catechism, for children. Julia had the chance to use it with her eight-year-old nephew Vespasiano, who came to live with her after her father died. Julia was overjoyed at this chance of caring for her nephew. She enjoyed walking and talking with him under the arches of the convent and listened with joy to his promises to live a Christian life, behave correctly, serve his prince, and never do anything shameful.

Julia enjoyed walking and talking with her nephew under the arches of the convent.

CHAPTER FIVE

Guardian of the Books

Sorrow reentered Julia's life in the summer of 1541, when her dear friend Valdés died of an illness at thirty-six years of age. In his will, he left all his writings to her care. Being in charge of these writings was a great responsibility, and Julia took it to heart, finding the right people to translate them from Spanish to Italian and financing their publication.

It was also a risky task. In 1542, the pope reopened a special court called Sacred Office of Inquisition, or simply Inquisition, to bring to trial anyone who disagreed with the teachings of the Roman Catholic Church. Julia had to be particularly careful because many portions of Valdés's books were close to the teachings of Protestants like Martin Luther. Also, there were always people ready to report others to the church authorities if it would help them win the pope's favor.

PAVLVS·III·PONT·MAX
M D XXXIIII
A·V

NATIONAL GALLERY OF ART, ROSENWALD COLLECTION

Paul III reopened the Sacred Office of Inquisition to stop Protestant teachings.

Julia sent instructions and support to the translators of Valdés's works.

In spite of these dangers, *Christian Alphabet* was published in 1545 in the Republic of Venice, a prosperous state that managed to stay independent from the pope. Julia also encouraged the publication of a book called *The Benefit of Christ*, which was also similar to Protestant books.

The Benefit of Christ was published without the name of the author in order to protect him from being killed, but Julia knew who it was: a monk named Benedetto (bey-ney-DEHT-toh), who had understood God's endless love for the church and His free gift of salvation through faith in Christ. This book was the first document to clearly explain these truths directly in Italian in a simple and poetic way that everyone could understand. It sold forty thousand copies within three months just in Venice—a huge number at that time.

Marcantonio Flaminio wrote and edited many books about the gospel. He was the editor of *The Benefit of Christ*.

Pietro Carnesecchi

Julia found much encouragement in her friends, especially a Florentine nobleman named Pietro (pee-AY-troh) Carnesecchi (kar-neh-SEHK-key), who had first met Julia in Fondi. Pietro, just a few years older than Julia, was also a follower of Valdés and found much comfort in her accounts of the gospel. Later in life, he said that her words opened up to him the kingdom of God.

Pietro lived for some time in Viterbo (vee-TEHR-boh), about sixty miles north of Rome, where a lively group of people shared his beliefs. He also spent a few years in Venice, which was a safe place for people who disagreed with the Roman Catholic Church. All along, he kept in close communication with Julia by mail and visited her often.

There was always much to write. In those days without newspapers and television, news traveled from person to person by letter or word of mouth. And there was a lot of news! Because of the Inquisition, some people had already left Italy, including the preacher Ochino.

Pietro wondered if he should leave too. Beyond the Alps there were Protestant churches influenced by the teachings of Reformers, such as Martin Luther and John Calvin, that shared Pietro's and Julia's beliefs. Each time, however, Pietro decided to stay a little longer, hoping the pope would understand that these beliefs agreed with the Scriptures. After all, there had been only one type of church in Western Europe for centuries, and reformers like Pietro didn't really want to leave it. They just wanted it to be more faithful to the Bible.

The situation became particularly scary in 1546, when Pietro was accused of rejecting the teachings of the Roman Catholic Church—a serious crime punishable by death. Thankfully, Cosimo (KO-zee-moe) I, ruler of Florence, liked Pietro and convinced the Inquisition to drop the charges.

Cosimo I de' Medici

NATIONAL GALLERY OF ART,
SAMUEL H. KRESS COLLECTION

Many people in Italy were opposed to the Inquisition. They thought especially the pope didn't have the right to arrest, imprison, and torture people who lived outside of his own state. In 1547, when the Spanish ruler of Naples joined the pope in bringing the harsher Spanish version of the Inquisition to that city, the people moved to the streets to fight back.

The rebellion lasted three months and ended with the death of six hundred Spaniards and two hundred Neapolitans. The Spanish army won, but the Inquisition in Naples was postponed. During the insurrection, Julia found refuge with a friend on the nearby island of Ischia (IS-kyah).

The castle of Costanza of Avalos, on the island of Ischia, where Julia stayed for a while.

TED STEVENS, FLICKR

In the meantime, Pietro found temporary relief by accepting a position at the French court of Queen Catherine de' Medici. In some ways, the situation in France was not safe either because the country was divided between Roman Catholics and Protestants and there were frequent fights. The pope, however, could not exercise as much power as he did in Italy and could not make direct arrests.

In 1551, it was Julia's turn to be alarmed when a notice by the Office of the Inquisition told her she was under investigation. She soon discovered why. A few months earlier, they had arrested a man who was thought to be a friend of Protestants and asked him for names of other believers. Afraid of being tortured and killed, the man had given the information they wanted. As soon as he was released, he fled to Switzerland. Julia's name was one of the few he had revealed.

Catherine de' Medici

NATIONAL GALLERY OF ART, GIFT OF JOHN O'BRIEN

Julia discovered she was under investigation.

In desperation, Julia asked her powerful cousin Ferrante and his brother Ercole (EHR-koh-ley), who was a Roman Catholic bishop, to help her, and they did. As Cosimo had done for Pietro, they were able to convince the officers of the Inquisition to drop their charges. Julia was not tried, but her name continued to appear in other investigations.

In spite of these troubles, she continued to promote the publication of books and to help her friends in every way she could. All over Italy she built a network of believers who were willing to house and protect those in danger. When she wrote about these things, she used a special code. Pietro was ++; Julia was 00. For other friends, she used different numbers or single letters.

Ferrante Gonzaga, Julia's cousin, was a military captain.

THE MET, HARRIS BRISBANE DICK FUND, 1936

CHAPTER SIX

Darker Skies

Every time a pope died, Julia and her friends hoped that the new one would bring about the change for which many Christians had been praying. In 1555, after the death of Pope Julius III, their hopes rose high. Cardinal Reginald Pole, who had been favorable to the Protestant Reformation, was in line to become pope. In the end, he lost by one vote, probably because his opponent, Gian Piero Carafa (JAHN PYEH-row kah-RAH-fah), the man who had been running the Inquisition, had spread rumors that Pole was Protestant.

With Carafa as pope, the practice of arresting people and destroying documents that questioned the teachings of the Roman Catholic Church intensified. Huge piles of books were taken to public squares and burned. This included all the books Julia had supervised and promoted.

Gian Piero Carafa, who became Pope Paul IV

NATIONAL GALLERY OF ART, GIFT OF ANDREW BROWN IN HONOR OF ELEONORA LUCIANO

Even two recent Italian translations of the Bible were destroyed. The pope was afraid the common people, by reading the Bible on their own, would come up with different interpretations from the Roman Catholic Church. He allowed only a Latin translation, which few people could read.

More Christians were arrested and imprisoned, including many of Julia's friends, such as her doctor and many of the nuns. Isabella Bresegna (bray-ZAY-nyah), a Spanish noblewoman whom Julia described as "the dearest friend I have," was forced to deny her faith. It was something Isabella had never meant to do. Deeply shaken, she decided to move to a Protestant country, even though it meant leaving her family behind. Julia gave her the money she needed for the journey and promised to send enough to support her every year. "May God be served as I help her," she said.

A copy of an Italian Bible, translated by Antonio Brucioli (brew-CHO-lee) and published in Venice in 1538. It was probably taken out of Italy, where it survived the fires of the Inquisition.

Julia said goodbye to her dear friend Isabella, giving her the money she needed for the journey.

Julia might have thought of leaving too, and it would have not been the first time. But she feared her sudden departure would place her friends in danger because the church would start suspecting everyone who had any contact with her.

In the meantime, Pietro, who had returned to Italy, was once again called to appear before the Inquisition. This time he simply refused to go, taking safety in Venice, which was, in his words, "Noah's ark in these troubled times." The church authorities decided to hold a trial without him and condemned him to death. Carafa, however, died just after that, and Pietro's execution was placed on hold.

Many people in Italy rejoiced at Carafa's death. As soon as the people in Rome discovered Carafa was dying, they started to run through the streets, burning down the building of the Inquisition and pulling down his statue. Then they cut off its head and threw it into the Tiber River. They also emptied the jail where the Inquisition had kept its religious prisoners.

The people of Rome set the Inquisition buildings on fire.

Thankfully, the new pope, Pius IV, was a friend of Cosimo and decided to pardon Pietro, who was able to return to Naples and visit Julia. In spite of this favor, the pope was not in agreement with Pietro's ideas.

Any hope the Roman Catholic Church would accept what Pietro and Julia believed was crushed in 1563, when a formal meeting of church leaders, called the Council of Trent, officially condemned those teachings. What's more, the Council declared that anyone who held to those beliefs was cursed by God.

For example, according to the Council, anyone who believed he could be saved only by believing in Christ, or anyone who said that God will keep believers faithful until the end was cursed by God.

These were all things Pietro and Julia had found clearly written in the Bible. And the list was much longer! Suddenly, Pietro, Julia, and all those who believed similar things were officially cursed by the church they had loved and tried to reform. What were they supposed to do?

Pius IV
NATIONAL ART GALLERY, SAMUEL H. KRESS COLLECTION

The Council's response was a natural reaction. The church leaders thought, "If we tell people that their sins are forgiven simply because Christ has paid for them on the cross and all they need to do is believe it, what would stop them from sinning even more? If we tell them that Christ clothes believers with His righteousness and they don't need to work hard to get to heaven, how can we get them to obey God?"

A sixteenth-century print of the Council of Trent

But Julia remembered what Valdés had taught her in their first conversation: when people understand what Christ has done for them, they want to obey Him! It is easier to obey someone out of love and thankfulness than out of fear.

Sadly, even some people who had understood these things switched sides at the end of the Council. Pietro had seen this happen many times before—people "changing their sails according to the winds." He compared the Roman Catholic Church to an unstable vessel. "Blessed are they who are outside this boat," he wrote, "as by the grace of God am I, both with my soul and my actions."

This situation confirmed something that Pietro and Julia had learned to appreciate, as he explained in a letter to her: "Our faith doesn't depend on men, nor is it founded on sand. It is founded on the living Rock, as it has been for the apostles, the prophets, and all the people God has chosen and made holy. May God give us grace to constantly live and die in that faith, for His glory."

More people left the country, while the Inquisition continued to make new arrests. Two of Pietro's friends were publicly burned alive in the Naples town square. Those who disagreed in any way with the Roman Catholic Church had to be extremely careful because the church encouraged people to report any suspect action or conversation. "There is no safety, not even in one's home," Pietro wrote, "because the son is expected to report his parents, the servant his master, the wife her husband, so much that people are now especially cautious around those who are closest."

Around the same time, Julia's health took a bad turn. We don't know the name of her illness, but it provoked low fevers, pain, and dizziness. Her doctors suggested that she move again to Ischia, where some hot springs were considered to be healing. She took their advice, even though she was not convinced of the waters' effect. "I am taking the waters more because of the opinion of others than because of the remedy," she wrote.

The hot springs of Cavascura, Ischia, were already famous to the ancient Romans. These waters start very hot at the spring and settle in natural pools inside the rock.

She tried other locations but finally went back to the convent in Naples. Realizing her remaining days were few, she wrote a last will, leaving her main properties to her nephew and some money to Isabella Bresegna, to the convent, and to her servants. By that time, Vespasiano was thirty-two and was ruling over many territories of both the Gonzaga and the Colonna families. He was still in touch with his aunt, but not too closely because he didn't share her beliefs and didn't want to be involved in her dangerous activities.

Julia must have been heartbroken to see her dear nephew reject the faith he had learned as a child. She shared her sorrow with Pietro, who reminded her "that it is God who plants." Parents have the duty to teach their children, but only God can plant the truth deep in their hearts and make it grow.

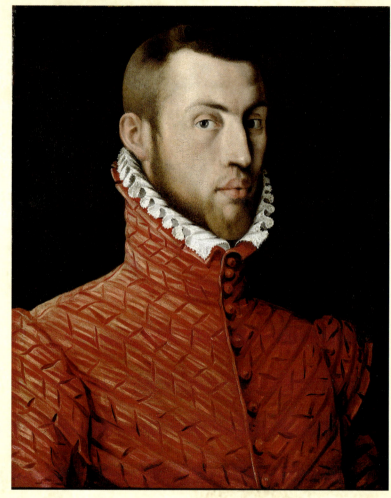

A statue of Vespasiano Gonzaga as a grown man
GALLERIA D'ORLANE

Pius V, the pope who most opposed Pietro Carnesecchi

THE WALTERS ART MUSEUM, BALTIMORE

Pietro could hardly bear the thought that Julia might die soon. "Do not think that I write this now with dry eyes," he said. "To live without you in this evil century is to navigate high seas without oars or sails."

He had, however, a feeling that he might not live much longer either. In December 1565, Pius IV died and was succeeded by a man who had strongly opposed Pietro's pardon and had continued to nurture suspicions against him. Taking the name of Pius V, the new pope reopened the investigations. "It may be that I will be unable to write anymore during my lifetime," Pietro wrote to Julia, "as there is a risk that I may be burned in Rome before departing for the next life."

Julia died peacefully on April 16, 1566. She was fifty-three. As predicted, Pietro found himself almost immediately in troubled seas. Just one month later, he received a letter from Vespasiano, telling him that the pope had sent his men to confiscate Julia's papers. Vespasiano was not worried. What could they find? He didn't know that Julia had kept many of the letters she had received. Of these, 228 were from Pietro.

The pope was glad to see those letters. Immediately, he realized he had enough proof to condemn both Julia and Pietro. "If I had seen them while she was still breathing," he said, "I would have burned her alive."

Pius V ordered the arrest of some of Julia's helpers. One servant managed to escape beyond the Alps. Pietro, who was in Florence, was arrested, imprisoned, and interrogated under torture. This time Duke Cosimo didn't protect him because the pope made some serious threats. Later, the duke felt sorry and tried to save Pietro, but it was too late. Eventually, the pope rewarded Cosimo by promoting him to the title of great duke.

Pietro was charged with believing things contrary to the Roman Catholic Church, befriending people who believed the same things, and reading banned books and writings. Since most of the Italian supporters of the Protestant ideas were dead or had left Italy, the questions focused on a few people who were still in the country. Pietro knew how important this information was for his accusers. If he had revealed what they wanted to know, he might have saved his life. Instead, he refused to do it, even under torture, in order to save his friends.

Julia's letters from Pietro were found in a papal search.

His death sentence was read on September 21, 1567, in front of a large group of church leaders. His execution happened ten days later in a small piazza, or square, before the bridge called Ponte Sant'Angelo. Being a nobleman, he was beheaded, which was considered a better death than burning. He dressed elegantly for the occasion, with a tight-fitting suit over a white shirt. His hands, covered by new gloves, held a white handkerchief. He looked so dignified that a man who reported the event called him "a man born to stand before kings."

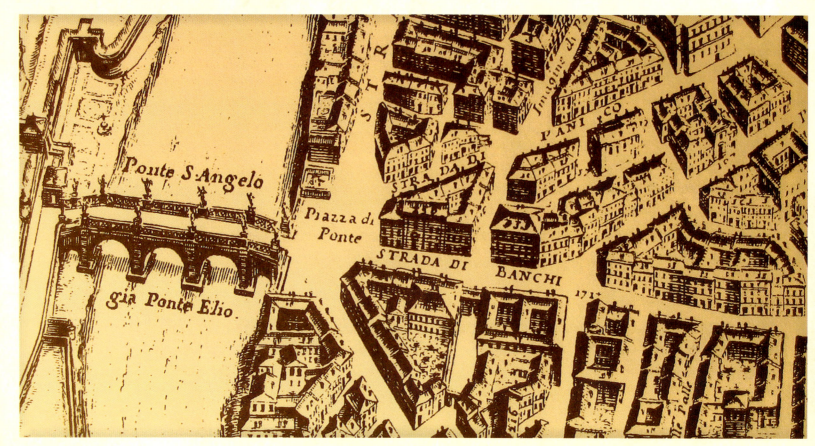

Piazza di Ponte

ALVARO DE ALVARIS

Pietro dressed elegantly for his execution.

The authorities made sure that Pietro's execution was well publicized, sending news everywhere as a warning to both Protestants and their supporters. They also searched for other people who were mentioned in Julia's letters. This new and stronger wave of threats and attacks silenced many Italians. But it was not the end. The same wave encouraged other people—nourished by the same gospel Julia had helped spread—to leave the country and join Protestant churches abroad. Many of these people became important theologians (people who study and write about God).

Italian Bibles continued to be outlawed inside the country until 1769, when a Roman Catholic translation of the Latin Bible was published. Sadly, most people in Italy didn't know how to read. Outside Italy, some Christians published Italian Bibles translated from the original Greek and Hebrew. They were more reliable because translations from the original languages are always better but were forbidden in Italy.

On September 20, 1870, the Italian army invaded Rome and put an end to the power of the pope as earthly ruler. To mark the occasion, a group of people entered Rome with a cartful of the new Italian Bibles. Today, Italy is still mostly Roman Catholic, but Italians are free to read any translation of the Bible, and the gospel can be preached without fear.

Time Line of Julia Gonzaga's Life

1513 — Julia Gonzaga is born at Gazzuolo, Italy.

1526 — Julia marries Vespasiano Colonna.

1528 — Vespasiano dies, and Julia takes over the administration of his lands.

1531 — Julia's brother Luigi marries Vespasiano's daughter, Isabella. They live with Julia and have a son, also called Vespasiano.

1532 — Luigi dies in battle.

1534 — Julia's properties are attacked by pirates. She escapes.

1536 — Julia moves to Naples, where she has a life-changing conversation with Juan de Valdés.

1540 — Julia adopts her nephew Vespasiano.

1541 — Juan de Valdés dies, and Julia takes over the publication and promotion of his books and similar writings.

1546 — Julia's friend Pietro Carnesecchi is accused of rejecting the teachings of the Roman Catholic Church.

1551 — The pope's special court announces that Julia is under investigation.

1555 — Gian Piero Carafa, the fiercest enemy of Protestants, becomes pope.

1563 — The Council of Trent ends.

1566 — Julia dies and her belongings are searched. Pietro's letters to her are found.

1567 — Pietro is executed by the Roman Catholic Church after a long period of torture and interrogations.

Did You Know?

Sixteenth-century girls like Julia, who were born in influential homes, learned all the skills that were necessary to entertain guests. Some learned to play the harpsichord, an older version of the piano.

Girls also learned to spin wool or flax (the fibers used to make linen), weave, and embroider in order to make clothes and nice objects. Often they took turns reading or playing an instrument while the others worked. Some favorite books at that time were stories of knights and damsels, including those about King Arthur's knights.

Favorite pastimes included watching plays (which were usually performed in their residences), walking in fields or gardens, horse riding, and playing chess or some sports such as tennis, with different rackets and rules than we have today. Some girls also enjoyed hunting. There were many dinners, parties, and tournaments to attend. According to her secretary, Julia loved to walk in the fields, admiring the different types of plants.

Normally boys received a higher education than girls. They also spent many hours learning to fight—mostly with swords and spears—and perfected their horse-riding skills. There were no formal schools, so most noble families hired tutors. Many preteens were sent to other families to learn under different tutors, meet new people, and create bonds. Bonds—or alliances—between families were very important at that time. That is why noble families made sure their sons and daughters married members of other important families.

❧ Fondi was a beautiful little town surrounded by olive groves, vineyards, and pastures for cows and sheep. It was also close to a swampy area full of malaria-carrying mosquitoes. Many robbers inhabited the forests, and the local streets were so badly maintained that a visitor advised travelers to bring along a doctor to fix their bones, a blacksmith to fix the horses' shoes, and a priest to bless the dying.

❧ Luigi Gonzaga was killed by a harquebus, a type of firearm invented in Spain in the fifteenth century. It was the first gun fired from the shoulder. Actually, it was so heavy that it often required a support. Gunfire arms were still a fairly recent invention and changed the way people fought.

❧ Many poets wrote about Julia, praising her beauty and virtues. Ludovico Ariosto, one of the greatest Italian poets of her time, sung her praises in his most celebrated book, *Orlando Furioso*:

> Wherever Iulia Gonzaga lays her foot,
> And wherever she turns her peaceful eye,
> Every other beauty to her capitulates
> As to a goddess descended from on high.

❧ Some experts believe that Costanza d'Avalos, Julia's friend who gave her hospitality on the island of Ischia during the popular rebellion in Naples, was Leonardo da Vinci's inspiration for the famous painting *Mona Lisa*. Costanza was a brave woman. After her husband died, she rallied her men against an invading French army and defeated them after a four-month struggle.

When Charles V defeated the fleet of pirate Khayr Al-Din in Tunisia, news circulated that the pirate was dead—to the joy of everyone in Western Europe. In reality, Khayr Al-Din managed to escape, joined another fleet he had left behind, and continued to raid the European islands and coasts. When he died, his memory was honored with a mausoleum, which is still in Instanbul (Constantinople's modern name).

The pope's campaign against Protestant writings was so successful that for centuries no one could find an Italian copy of *The Benefit of Christ*, which was published with Julia's support. The only surviving copy was found in 1855 at St. John's College Library in Cambridge, England.

Still, no one knew who the author was until 1881, when Pope Leo XIII allowed the Vatican Secret Archives to be opened to researchers. These archives included a long transcription of Carnesecchi's trial, where he revealed that the *Benefit of Christ* was written by a monk known as Benedetto da Mantua. Carnesecchi could reveal Benedetto's name because the monk had died ten years earlier.

Italians who, like Julia, wanted to help the church return to the basic teachings of the Bible were often called *spirituali*, to show how much they cared for spiritual matters. The famous artist Michelangelo Buonarroti became involved with a group of *spirituali*, particularly through one of their main supporters, the poetess Vittoria Colonna. Michelangelo's contact with the *spirituali* and his understanding of the gospel as a message of salvation by grace alone and through faith alone affected many of his later works, including paintings, sculptures, and poems.

Sixteenth-century Venice was a refuge for people who wanted to think freely and explore ideas that the Roman Catholic Church didn't allow. Because of its flourishing business by sea, the Republic of Venice was rich and powerful enough to keep independent from the oppressive authority of both pope and emperor.

In fact, in 1605, Venice came close to becoming a Protestant country. It all started when the Venetian authorities arrested two clergymen who had been accused of common crimes and the pope asked that they be sent to Rome instead. The Venetians didn't think it was right. They thought the crime had to be punished and that the pope wanted to cover it up instead. When they refused to hand over the criminals, the pope excommunicated the whole city. That means no priest was authorized to perform religious services. In reality, most of the priests sided with the Venetian government and continued their services as usual.

Eventually, this became an international matter, with England on the side of Venice, and Spain and Austria on the side of the pope. Finally, a year later, the French authorities brought the two factions to a compromise: the two clergymen were delivered to France, which in turn delivered them to the church. It was a victory for Rome, but Venice was able to stand by its convictions.

Some influential people in Venice began to insist that the city should make a permanent break from Rome, becoming Protestant instead. One of the supporters of this idea became a victim of two attempted murders by men who found refuge in the pope's territories. In the end, however, the Venetian government decided they were not ready for such a drastic action.

Many Italians who understood the message of salvation by grace alone and through faith alone were convinced that the pope would eventually agree, so they stayed in Italy even when things became dangerous. Most Protestants outside of Italy, however, disagreed with their decision, which usually forced them to hide their beliefs. The French Reformer John Calvin coined a nickname for these people: Nicodemites, from the name of Nicodemus, a Pharisee who visited Jesus at night because he didn't want people to see him. He encouraged these Italians to leave Italy and go where they could worship freely.

🌸 Education flourished in Protestant countries, where the common people were encouraged to read the Bible. In 1861 only 25 percent of the people in Italy and Spain, both strong Roman Catholic countries, could read and write, as opposed to 69 percent in England; 80 percent in the United States, Germany, Austria, and Switzerland; and 90 percent in Scandinavia.

🌸 Living inside a convent was a common choice for widows like Julia. Quite often convents included libraries where the nuns could further their education. In order to live there without becoming a nun, however, women had to get special permission from the pope.

In 1568, after Julia's death, Pope Pius V turned the convent where she had stayed into a *cloistered convent*, which means that the nuns who lived there were no longer allowed to have any contact with the world outside, apart from their own families.

Julia's Voice

The few writings by Julia that have survived are mostly about practical matters. Unlike Julia, who kept her correspondence, Pietro was careful to destroy all the letters she sent him. We still have her comments and questions in the conversation she had with Juan de Valdès in 1536. This conversation helps us see what was on her mind and how Valdès was able to help her. Here are two portions:

Julia: Come on now, let's come to the heart of the matter. Tell me what you think about this conflict I feel inside.

Valdès: I'll say, my lady, that while I have compassion for you and feel sorry that you have to live with the confusion we have just discussed, I am also glad and pleased to hear of this conflict.

Julia: Why?…

Valdès: Because it is a sign that you have listened to the teachings. Even if the preaching didn't work in you the way the preacher originally intended, I am glad that at least the law was able to perform its task. Now I hope that, by God's grace, the gospel will also perform its task.

Julia: I think I understand what you mean, but I would like to understand a little more, particularly about the task of the law and the task of the gospel.

Valdès: It is very good for you, my lady, to understand both…. When God gave the law to Moses, the people of Israel who were at the foot of the mountain heard great thunder and lightning flashes, so that they all trembled with fear—and everyone says this signifies the terror, fright, and inner conflict the law creates in the hearts of the people who receive it. But you should also know, my lady, that the law is very necessary because without the law there wouldn't be a conscience, and without a conscience we wouldn't know our sin, and without knowing our sin we would not humble ourselves, and without humbling ourselves we would not receive grace, and without grace we would not be justified, and without justification our souls would not be saved. This is the task of the law. At the same time, the gospel works in those who see it, not as law but as messenger of grace and peace. It has the task of healing the wounds inflicted by the law; preaching grace, peace, and remission of sins; calming and pacifying consciences; imparting the spirit that allows us to keep what the law shows about God's will; and to fight, conquer, and crush the enemies of our souls.

★ ★ ★ ★ ★ ★

Julia: I understand, and I would like for you to tell me, without flatteries, if you can lead me on a path where I can follow your directions…because I have a strong tendency to follow my own desires, as you must have noticed….

Valdès: I will be glad to, but first tell me if you have ever crossed a river on foot.

Julia: I have. Many times.

Valdès: Did you notice how, if you look in the water, you feel dizzy, so much that if you don't catch yourself and fix your eyes on the other side of the river, you could fall and run the danger of drowning?

Julia: Yes, I have.

Valdès: And did you see how, by keeping your eyes fixed on the other shore, you can avoid these feelings and this danger?

Julia: I have seen this too.

Valdès: So, my lady, if you want to cross the river of the things of this world, make sure you don't look at them with affection, or you'll end up like those who look at the water, fall, and drown. Make sure the eyes of your soul are always fixed and secure on the crucified Christ. Anytime you forget this and start looking at the things of this world so much that you feel a pull toward them, catch yourself and place your eyes back on the crucified Christ.

Acknowledgments

I hesitated before writing this book. Julia Gonzaga is not well known, and I have written other books on the Reformation. So, my first thanks go to my pastor, Rev. Michael Brown, who thought this would be a needed addition to the series. He thought it was important for children to see how many people in Italy, the land of the pope, felt a need for a reformation of the church and how long they had to go without an Italian Bible when that reformation didn't take place.

I owe a huge debt of thanks to Dr. Susanna Peyronel Rambaldi, professor of modern history and history of the Reformation and Counter-Reformation at the State University of Milan, Italy, and author of *Una gentildonna irrequieta. Giulia Gonzaga fra reti familiari e relazioni eterodosse* (A restless gentlewoman: Giulia Gonzaga between family networks and heterodox relations). Dr. Rambaldi has devoted much of her time to my book, reading the manuscript, answering my questions, and offering valuable suggestions.

As usual, I am grateful to my friends Ellie Charter, Dianna Ippolito, and Rebecca Richards, who have read the manuscript and provided much encouragement and advice. My faithful team of young readers has included Trinity Brindis de Salas; Emma James; Lucas and Linus Plotner; Isaiah, Jaelyn, and Adri Hasten; Hannah and Ava Lo; and Lok and Kai Mendelez. Their interest in this book and their insightful questions have been particularly helpful.

Many thanks go once again to my husband and children and to my church family for their constant support, as well as to my exceptional artist, Matt Abraxas; his wife, Rebecca (who posed as Julia); and everyone who has provided photos.

The final product would not have been possible without the vision and backing of my publisher, Dr. Joel Beeke; and the director of publications, Jay Collier; nor without the diligent editing of Annette Gysen and the creative skills of the staff at Reformation Heritage Books.